Popular Culture:
2000 and Beyond

Nick Hunter

Raintree is an imprint of Capstone Global Library
Limited, a company incorporated in England and Wales
having its registered office at 7 Pilgrim Street, London,
EC4V 6LB – Registered company number: 6695582

Text © Capstone Global Library Limited 2013
First published in hardback in 2013
The moral rights of the proprietor have been asserted.

Edited by Adam Miller, Andrew Farrow, and
  Adrian Vigliano
Designed by Richard Parker
Original illustrations © Capstone Global Ltd 2013
Illustrations by Richard Parker
Picture research by Mica Brancic
Originated by Capstone Global Library Ltd
Printed and bound in China by Leo Paper Products Ltd

ISBN 978 1 406 24025 2
16 15 14 13 12
10 9 8 7 6 5 4 3 2 1

British Library Cataloguing in Publication Data
A full catalogue record for this book is available from
the British Library.

Acknowledgments
We would like to thank the following for permission to
reproduce photographs: Alamy p. 51 (© incamerastock);
Getty Images pp. 4 (National Geographic/Annie
Griffiths Belt), 7 (AFP Photo/Mehdi Fedouach), 8 (AFP
Photo/Liu Jin), 15 (Ian Gavan), 13 (Paramount Pictures/
Alberto E. Rodriguez), 17 (FilmMagic/ Jeff Kravitz), 20
(Echo), 25 (Bloomberg/Tony Avelar), 27 (AFP Photo),
31 (WireImage/Steve Granitz), 33 (Neilson Barnard),
49 (Andreas Rentz), 29 (Tim Boyle), 35 (WireImage/
Kevin Mazur), 22 (Michael Grecco), 37 (FilmMagic), 39
(ChinaFotoPress), 38 (Matt Cardy), 41 (Jim Dyson), 47
(Alexandra Beier), 45 (Tim Robberts), 44 (Bloomberg/
Gino Domenico), 52 (AFP Photo/Emmanuel Dunand),
40 (Indigo), 43 (UpperCut Images/David Burch), 46
(David Livingston); Photoshot pp. 10 (© Face to Face),
11 (© Copyright 2001 by Courtesy of Disney/Pixar);
Press Association Images pp. 19 (AP Photo/Rene
Macura), 32 (AP Photo/Mark Lennihan); Rex Features
p. 26 (KeystoneUSA-ZUMA); White House flickr p.
9. Background images and design features reproduced
with permission of Shutterstock.

Cover photograph of crowds of young fans at Pinkpop
Festival in Landgraaf, Netherlands reproduced with
the permission of Getty Images (Redferns/© 2011 Paul
Bergen).

Contents

What is popular culture? 4

A turbulent decade 6

Films 10

TV and home entertainment 16

Online pop culture 22

The age of celebrity 30

Music 34

Design and clothes..40

The printed word 44

Pop culture turned upside down?....................48

What did the 2000s do for us?........................50

Timeline..54

Best of the era..56

Notes on sources..57

Find out more..60

Glossary..62

Index...64

Some words are printed in bold, **like this**. You can find out what they mean by looking in the glossary.

What is popular culture?

In June 2007, a line of people snaked around three sides of a city block in New York City. It was a diverse group of people. Many of them had waited for hours or even days. Many had travelled from other countries to join the line. At 6 p.m. on 29 June, the doors would open and the throng of people would scramble to get their hands on the object of their affections.[1]

Sydney, Australia, celebrates on 1 January 2000. People around the world celebrated the start of a new millennium with optimism about the future, but few could have foreseen the changes that would come in society and culture.

What were they waiting for? Was it a rare appearance by a film or music star, or a scramble for tickets to a one-off show or sporting event that they could not possibly miss? The fact that many were clutching laptop computers gave passers-by a clue. These people were waiting for the launch of the iPhone, the latest "must-have" **gadget** from Apple. They had to get there ahead of everyone else, even though the phone would be widely available and, over the following years, millions would be sold.

In the twenty-first century, gadgets like the iPhone have become part of pop culture. Just like reading the latest bestselling book or seeing the current **blockbuster** film, many people seek to own the latest technology. Pop, or popular, culture includes anything that is designed to entertain or enrich the lives of as many people as possible. Pop culture includes films, music, magazines, and even advertisements. Even the design styles of products such as cars and mobile phones can be part of pop culture, because they are produced to appeal to people as being desirable as well as useful objects.

Time of change

The early twenty-first century has seen massive changes to popular culture, with the Internet revolutionizing music, books, and the way people interact, creating whole new forms of pop culture and ways of making it instantly available to millions of people. Many of these changes began in the 1990s, but the pace of change was even more astonishing in the first decade of the new **millennium**.

The Internet explosion

Internet use increased dramatically around the world after the year 2000. In 2000, only about 6 per cent of the world's people were Internet users. In 2011, the figure was 30 per cent. The change in some regions of the world was even more dramatic. More than half of the Internet users in 2000 were in North America and Europe. In 2011, there were almost one billion people online in Asia, making up almost half of the total.[2] The way people use the Internet has also changed. More people have high-speed and wireless connections so they can be online at any time, anywhere in the world.

A turbulent decade

Pop culture reflects what is happening in society at the time it is made. The year 2000 started with a wave of optimism. Much of the world was nearing the peak of a dot-com boom as the Internet became part of everyday life. This optimism started to fade in the second half of 2000 when many Internet companies started to fail. It was brought to a shattering end on 11 September 2001, when **radical Islamist** terrorists hijacked four passenger jets, crashing two of them into New York's World Trade Center, another into the Pentagon building near Washington, DC, and a fourth in a field in Pennsylvania. Almost 3,000 people died in the attacks.[1]

War on terror

US president George W. Bush vowed to pursue a war on terror to defeat terrorists. US troops began an invasion of Afghanistan, where the Taliban government was sheltering Osama Bin Laden and other leaders of the Al-Qaeda terrorist organization. The United States was supported by the United Kingdom and other allies who were appalled by the attacks. The war continued for more than a decade, even after the killing of Bin Laden by US forces in 2011.

While the war in Afghanistan was seen as a direct consequence of the 9/11 attacks, Bush's next war, to remove Saddam Hussein from power in Iraq, was much less popular. People questioned the reasons for the war and whether it was legal. The war also provoked more terrorist attacks, particularly on the people of Iraq, but also on the streets of international cities such as London and Madrid. These wars and **terrorism** were **themes** of a lot of pop culture during this period.

Financial crash

Despite the threat of war and terrorism, economies continued to boom. Homeowners in prosperous Western countries felt they were better off as prices of property rose, and bankers in the big financial centres such as the City of London and Wall Street were taking home million-pound bonuses. When it became clear from 2007 onwards that many of these bonuses were based on lending money to people who couldn't afford to pay it back, the financial system crashed and the world was plunged into economic crisis.

At the end of the decade, US voters elected the first African American president. He took over a country at war and in economic crisis, but Barack Obama's election was still seen by some as the culmination of a struggle for racial **equality** that had been a feature of much of twentieth-century culture.

The war in Iraq divided opinion between those who thought it was necessary and those who opposed it. Books, films, and online media explored many aspects of the conflict.

Pop culture in the face of terrorism

Following the 9/11 attacks, some Hollywood films were delayed or cancelled because film-makers felt that people would be offended by fictional terrorism in the face of the horrifying reality of the attacks. Films about 9/11, such as *United 93* (2006), followed a few years later. In the meantime, US-led invasions of Afghanistan and Iraq, and concerns about human-rights abuses in the treatment of prisoners, led many in popular culture to question the actions of the US, the UK, and their allies.

Globalization

Another feature of world affairs in the early years of the twenty-first century was the growing prominence of Asian countries. As Western economies struggled with the economic crisis, the economies of China, India, and other countries in Asia kept getting stronger. With populations of more than one billion people each, China and India became increasingly important in manufacturing and other industries. As their wealth grew, they began to challenge Western countries as **consumers**, including as consumers of popular culture.

Economic success has increased the gap between rich and poor among China's population. A wealthy middle class has emerged in China's cities.[2]

Technology and industry

Technology played a vital role in the development of this new global economy, partly because the Internet made instant communication possible with businesses on the other side of the world. Developments in technology also meant that computers and other devices became smaller, more powerful, and also less expensive. This meant that high-tech items like large-screen televisions and **smartphones** were affordable to the mass population. Even crime was affected, because prices of items such as DVD players dropped so low that they weren't worth stealing.[3]

Clothes, toys, and other products that were often made in China became so cheap that they were almost **disposable**. **Pollution** from discarded goods and packaging was one environmental problem affecting the world. More disturbing was the continuing evidence that Earth's climate was getting warmer and that humans needed to do something to reduce emissions of **greenhouse gases** into the atmosphere as a result of industry and the burning of **fossil fuels** like oil. As governments discussed the best ways to tackle this potential catastrophe, it became a major debate within pop culture.

Freedom of speech

Many artists in Western popular culture take for granted that they will be able to say whatever they like. In many countries this is not the case. In China, films that criticize the government are not allowed. In many countries free access to the Internet is also restricted.

Barack Obama (1961–)

Barack Obama (shown here with his family watching the 2011 Women's World Cup final) made history on 20 January, 2009, when he was sworn in as the first African American president of the United States. Obama was born in Hawaii and spent part of his childhood in Indonesia. He later returned to Hawaii and was largely brought up by his grandparents. After attending college, Obama moved to Chicago, Illinois, where he worked as a community organizer before practising as a lawyer. In 2004, he was elected as a US senator for Illinois. His successful campaign to become president was based on his charisma and appeal to voters looking for change after the presidency of Republican George W. Bush. His campaign also used social media effectively to win support. In 1992, he married Michelle Robinson, and the couple had two children, Malia and Sasha.[4]

Films

People still went to the cinema in the twenty-first century, although they had more opportunities to watch feature films in other ways than ever before. Films were usually available on DVD, television, or **download** soon after they had been shown in the cinemas. For many people the social experience of going to the cinema with friends or family is worthwhile. It is also difficult to match the experience of seeing a film on the big screen, especially dramatic, highly visual films like many of the biggest successes of this period.

Computer-generated blockbusters

The kinds of films people bought tickets to see were certainly changing. Special effects have been part of cinema since the earliest films, but blockbusters came to be dominated by **computer-generated imagery (CGI)**. This changed the rules on what directors could film. Some of the most successful films in the early part of the decade were *The Lord of the Rings* trilogy (2001–2003), based on J. R. R. Tolkien's much-loved fantasy novels. CGI was combined with the dramatic landscapes of New Zealand to bring Tolkien's fantasy world to life. The technique of **motion capture** was also used to give the animated creature Gollum the realistic movement of actor Andy Serkis.

Like many big-budget animated films, *Monsters, Inc.* (2001) features the voices of Hollywood stars such as John Goodman and Billy Crystal.

Some of the most popular blockbusters seemed to be about more than just the film on the screen. Young and old viewers alike were entranced by amazing animated films such as the four *Shrek* films and the third installment in the *Toy Story* series. These films were not just about selling cinema tickets or even DVDs, but also about selling a huge range of merchandise, from figures of the characters to bags and T-shirts. The *Harry Potter* series was another huge multimedia franchise that triumphed at the **box office**.

Did you know?

Avatar was one of the most expensive films ever made. The cost of production was estimated at around $280 million, but that did not include the 3-D cameras and motion capture technology that were developed specially for the film.[1]

James Cameron's *Avatar* (2009) used amazing CGI effects to become the most successful film of all time.

The 3-D revival

As films became more widely available for home viewing, studios and cinemas looked for new ways to attract people. Three-dimensional films had been popular briefly in the 1950s, and special IMAX cinemas had started showing **3-D** films, such as *The Polar Express* (2004).[2] Later in the decade, many films began to be released in 3-D, particularly children's animated films, such as *Up*. Viewers had to wear special glasses to see the effects. Some, such as the very successful *Avatar*, were shot using 3-D cameras, but these were very expensive to make and many films were converted to 3-D after shooting.[3] Many people felt that 3-D added little to the film and its popularity with film companies was due to the fact that studios and cinemas could charge more for each ticket to see a 3-D film.

Fading film stars?

For decades, film actors had been the biggest stars in the world, but many films in the 2000s were successful because they were part of a **brand** rather than because of who the stars were. Daniel Radcliffe, who starred as Harry Potter in the series of films based on the children's books, was unknown when he was selected for this role. The first film in the series, *Harry Potter and the Philosopher's Stone* (2001), was bound to be successful because of the popularity of the books and the amount of money that was spent **marketing** the film. However, the high quality of acting by Radcliffe and his co-stars helped ensure that people would keep coming back for the next film in the series.

The success of films as brands did not mean the end of the film star. Johnny Depp was one actor who could almost guarantee that a film would be a success, particularly when combined with a successful brand such as the *Pirates of the Caribbean* series. Brad Pitt and Angelina Jolie also established themselves as some of the biggest stars in Hollywood. New stars to emerge included Robert Pattinson and Keira Knightley.

African American winners

African American actors also saw success during this decade. In 2001, Halle Berry became the first African American to win the best actress award at the annual **Oscars** award ceremony. At the same ceremony, African American Denzel Washington was named best actor. Jamie Foxx triumphed in 2004 for his portrayal of musician Ray Charles, and Will Smith continued his progress to become one of the world's biggest film stars.

Documentary films

Documentary films are factual films about a particular subject. The early 2000s saw the release of some successful documentary films, as well as fictionalized retellings of real events. These documentaries were often critical of government or corporations, such as Michael Moore's *Fahrenheit 9/11* (2004) about the terrorist attacks of 2001, and Morgan Spurlock's *Super Size Me* (2004), which looked at the health dangers of fast food. Even former US vice president Al Gore had success with the film *An Inconvenient Truth* (2006) about global warming. These documentaries appeared on cinema screens because of limited time for this form of film on mainstream TV and because they often expressed strong, and not very balanced, views on controversial topics.

Will Smith (1968–)

Before becoming one of Hollywood's most famous faces, Will Smith already had a successful music and TV career as the Fresh Prince. After growing up in Philadelphia, Pennsylvania, he teamed up with school friend Jazzy Jeff to make poppy hip-hop hits like "Parents Just Don't Understand" (1987), and he starred in the very successful TV series *The Fresh Prince of Bel-Air* (1990–1996). Smith's first successful Hollywood movie was *Bad Boys* (1995). Since then he has starred in huge hit films such as *Men in Black* (1997), *I, Robot* (2004), *I Am Legend* (2007), and *Hancock* (2008). He married Jada Pinkett in 1997, and the couple's two children, Jaden and Willow, are building their own careers in acting and music.[4]

Bollywood

India is one of the major centres of world film-making. Many Indians do not have a television at home, so the cinema remains their main source of entertainment. During the 2000s, as India's prosperity and influence increased and Indian communities grew in many cities from Birmingham, UK, to San Francisco, California, films made in the country were being watched around the world. The films of Bollywood were particularly popular and started to have an influence outside India.

Bollywood is the name given to the Hindi-language film industry based in India's largest city, Mumbai (previously called Bombay). There are films made in other Indian cities, such as Kolkata, but Bollywood became the centre of a particular type of film that combines romance, comedy, and action sequences with elaborate dancing and music.

However, Bollywood films also adapted to reflect the changes in India itself. Action and adventure films similar to those made in Hollywood started to become a bigger part of the Bollywood mix. Films also looked at class and other social issues in the new India.

Bollywood's stars

Bollywood's leading stars are hugely popular in India, and their fame is spreading around the world. Along with the older **generation** of established stars, including the legendary Amitabh Bachchan and Shahrukh Khan, there are many younger stars who have found fame in Bollywood's more recent films, including Aamir Khan and John Abraham. Female stars include Aishwarya Rai, Katrina Kaif, and Kareena Kapoor.

The 2000s saw many successful Bollywood films that raised the profile of Indian films with Western audiences, including *Lagaan* and *Monsoon Wedding*, both from 2001, and *Devdas* from 2002.[5]

Did you know?

India's film industry produces around 1,000 films every year, more than any other country.[6] Indians also buy more cinema tickets than any other nation.[7]

Influence outside India

Bollywood's influence could be seen in many Western films in the 2000s. Baz Luhrmann's *Moulin Rouge* (2001) borrowed many elements from traditional Bollywood films. Gurinder Chadha's *Bend It Like Beckham* (2002), about a Sikh girl in the United Kingdom who longs to play football, featured some Bollywood-style scenes. Chadha's *Bride and Prejudice* went one step further by moving the story from Jane Austen's *Pride and Prejudice* novel to an Indian setting. Bollywood's most visible influence on Western film came in 2008 when *Slumdog Millionaire*, Danny Boyle's tale of young people escaping from the slums of Mumbai, won the Oscar for Best Picture. The film featured many established Indian stars.

Aishwarya Bachchan Rai (1973–)

Aishwarya Rai did not plan to become a film star at all. She was training to be an architect when she won the Miss World title in 1994. Modelling contracts followed, and in 1997 Rai starred in her first film, *Iruvar*. Rai's early films were part of a new style of film in Bollywood that broke with many of the formulas of the past. Rai established herself as the Queen of Bollywood with her performance in *Devdas* (2002). Her fame spread around the world when the film was screened at the Cannes Film Festival. Her first English-language film was the Bollywood-inspired *Bride and Prejudice* (2004). In 2007, Aishwarya Rai married Abhishek Bachchan, from one of Bollywood's most famous families. The couple starred together in *Raavan* (2010).[8]

Game consoles

In 2000, Sony launched PlayStation 2 (PS2). This was a major step forward for the gaming industry, as the new console had better graphics capability than had been available previously. Games were available on the relatively new DVD format, which had much more storage than CD-ROMs.[6] In 2001, the Nintendo GameCube and Microsoft's Xbox were also launched.[7] At the same time, an earlier generation of gamers was becoming parents. Console gaming was established as part of home entertainment for the whole family, not just children and teenagers.

Nintendo aimed the Wii at families, with the emphasis on uncontroversial subjects and active games that would promote fitness.

The next major step forward came with the launch of the Xbox 360 in 2005, and the Nintendo Wii and PlayStation 3 in 2006.[8] The Wii was particularly distinctive with its motion-sensing features that enabled users to **simulate** sports such as tennis with the console's game controllers.

The best-selling console games of all time, as of 2011, were all produced after 2007. Popular games included the *Call of Duty* series, the music games *Rock Band* and *Guitar Hero*, and Nintendo's *Wii Fit* and other sport simulators.[9]

Online gaming

Online games started to appear in the mid-1990s. They were also called **MMORPGs (massively multiplayer online role-playing games)**. Early MMORPGs such as *Ultima Online* and *EverQuest* involved groups of players working together. The next generation of games was more suited to solo play, including *Star Wars Galaxies*, launched in 2001, and *World of Warcraft* (2004), which became the most successful game of all. Virtual social worlds like *Second Life* also became popular.[10]

Gaming under fire

Many of the most popular video games, such as the *Grand Theft Auto* and *Call of Duty* series, were accused of being excessively violent. Debate has raged about whether this can harm players or affect their attitudes towards violence. In many countries, games are rated in a similar way to films to prevent shops from selling violent games to young people. Online gaming has also raised the question of Internet safety. Someone playing an online game may not be who they say they are, and there have been examples of online predators posing as teenagers online to build friendships with young players. You should always be aware of this when chatting to people online and never arrange to meet someone you meet online.

Did you know?

America's Army is one of the most popular online games. The game was developed by the US Army in 2002. It is available free of charge and aims to attract recruits by giving them a realistic sense of the training and skills of a US Army soldier.[11] The game is controversial because it uses popular culture for political ends and presents a completely positive view of working in the military.

Online pop culture

Online gaming was just one aspect of the impact of the Internet on popular culture around the world. In 2000, many of the websites and applications that became a vital part of many people's lives a decade later were in their infancy or did not exist at all. Access to the Internet from home was usually by a slow dial-up connection, with only about 200,000 broadband users in the United Kingdom by 2002.[1] The idea of connecting to the Internet wirelessly was still being developed.[2]

The rise of Google

At the start of 2000, Google Inc. was two years old. Its new kind of search engine was popular with those who knew about it, and it made around seven million searches every day.[3] In 2000, the company started to include advertising as part of search results and providing searches for Yahoo! Inc. By the end of 2000, Google was making 100 million searches per day and was well on its way to becoming one of the companies that would dominate the Internet. The verb to *google* entered the Oxford English Dictionary in 2006, and you don't need this book to tell you what it means![4] As well as searches, Google provided email and services such as Google Earth, which enabled users to see an aerial view of anywhere on Earth. Google's impact on all areas of popular culture was assured when it bought the video-sharing website YouTube in 2006.[5]

Google's founders Larry Page and Sergey Brin began to develop their idea for a new search engine while they were graduate students at Stanford University.

The changing Web

The World Wide Web was not just bigger and busier at the end of the decade than it had been in 2000; it was also very different. In 2000, the Web for many people was primarily a great source of information and a place to shop for everything from books to holidays. By the end of the decade, the Web still did those things but had become much more about people creating their own content. Wikipedia, launched in 2001,[6] was a huge online encyclopedia, created and edited by its users. Anyone could communicate to the world using their own websites or by contributing to forums.

The blogosphere

Blogs (short for "Web log") allowed people to write and easily publish their own thoughts and ideas. By the summer of 2011, there were more than 160 million blogs.[7] The best-known blogs attracted millions of visitors and became hugely influential. Bloggers' influence ranged from news and reviews of new technology and gadgets to celebrity gossip, in which often anonymous bloggers could react more quickly to celebrity stories, and often with more irreverent or even nasty comments than the mainstream media would allow. Blogging became very important in politics, with blogs such as the *Huffington Post* growing into online newspapers.

Some of the most popular websites in 2010 did not even exist in 2000.

The world's most popular websites

Site	No. of visitors
Google (Search and portal site)	350 million unique visitors
MSN/WindowsLive/Bing (Search and portal site)	272 million
Yahoo! (Search and portal site)	233 million
Microsoft (Computing and software)	220 million
Facebook (Social network)	218 million
YouTube (Video sharing)	203 million
Wikipedia (Reference)	154 million
AOL (Search and portal site)	128 million
eBay (Retail)	122 million
Apple (Computing and software)	119 million

Figures from Nielsen for January 2010 for selected countries[8]

Social networks

By 2010, the social network had become the main way for people to interact online. Of course, connecting and communicating with friends had always been part of the Internet. In the late 1990s, people started to realize the social possibilities of the Web. Sites such as classmates.com, launched in 1995, and later the UK site Friends Reunited helped people to get in touch with old school and college friends. They were followed by Friendster (2002), which took the concept of creating an online network of friends a bit further.

In August 2003,[9] MySpace was launched. This was a new kind of social networking site that enabled users to share more than just their basic profile information. MySpace became a favourite for musicians to post their new material online, and bands such as the Arctic Monkeys gained large online followings. By 2005, the site was adding 70,000 new users per day and was bought by Rupert Murdoch's giant media corporation NewsCorp.[10]

The Facebook phenomenon

The year 2004 also saw the launch of Facebook. It did not become available for use outside North American colleges until 2006, but it soon established itself as a competitor for MySpace. It was simple, easy to use, and wasn't clogged up with the advertising that was becoming a bigger part of MySpace.

In the wake of Facebook, new social networks developed that were slightly different. YouTube was already well established for sharing and viewing videos. Twitter and Tumblr enabled users to "microblog" short messages to followers and follow the "tweets" of others. Barack Obama used many of these tools to build support during his election campaign of 2008.

The enormous popularity of Facebook and other networks changed the way people communicated with each other. People used Facebook to meet new friends, start campaigns, or communicate with a wider audience. They became part of popular culture because people were spending more of their leisure time on social networks rather than watching TV or reading a magazine, which they might have done in the past.

Quote

"I'm trying to make the world a more open place."
Facebook founder Mark Zuckerberg, 20 September 2010[11]

Mark Zuckerberg (1984-)

Mark Zuckerberg is one of the world's youngest billionaires. He launched Facebook in 2004 with a group of friends while studying at Harvard University. The site expanded to other North American colleges and eventually to any user with an email address in 2006.[12] By 2010, Facebook had 500 million registered users. Despite his success, Zuckerberg has faced criticism. Former colleagues have accused him of being ruthless in taking control of Facebook. The film *The Social Network* (2010) told Facebook's story and did not always give a flattering portrait of Zuckerberg.[13]

Phones

The first decade of the twenty-first century was when the mobile phone became an essential part of almost everyone's life, and not just in the affluent Western world. In 2000, mobile phones were used primarily to make phone calls or send SMS text messages. By the middle of the decade, mobile phones typically included cameras and limited Web browsing.

People began to use their phones in the same way as they might have used a home computer in the past, gaining access to the Web and email and playing music. In 2007, Apple launched the iPhone.[14] This ushered in the age of the smartphone and, for many people, ended the era of the mobile phone. Smartphones could make calls, but they were in effect mini-computers. Software developers were able to create small applications, or apps, for smartphones, so users could add games, news feeds, and much more.

The Apple effect

The iPhone was not the only Apple product to become a pop culture icon in the 2000s. Apple computers had been pioneers of the personal computer in the 1980s, but by the late 1990s their popularity lay with a relatively small group of enthusiasts, especially when compared to the dominance of the PC running Windows software developed by Microsoft. In 2001, Apple launched a product that would change the way people listened to music forever. The iPod was not the first MP3 player, but its storage capacity and simple, attractive design meant that it appealed to people who had never thought of needing an MP3 player.[15]

By 2011, more than 100 million iPhones had been sold around the world. Users had also downloaded more than 10 billion apps.[16]

Internet memes

With more people connected more of the time through computers, phones, and other devices, the power of the Internet to spread ideas and images to a huge audience very quickly became a feature of pop culture. **Internet memes** are ideas, including images and video clips that can be circulated to millions of people by email and links in blogs. They were a new feature of pop culture in the 2000s. One of the most famous is the supposed video blog of Lonelygirl15. The filmed thoughts of "Bree" were first posted on YouTube in 2006, attracting millions of viewers. It was later discovered that "Bree" was an actress with a scriptwriter.[17]

Mobile phones and the Internet also helped people to communicate news stories to the wider world, such as in this picture of anti-government protests in Syria in 2011.

Did you know?

In 2000, little more than 1 in 10 of the world's population owned a mobile phone.[18] In 2010, there were five billion phone connections, or a phone for 7 out of 10 people. The Asia-Pacific region, including India and China, accounted for almost half of all connections.[19]

Disruptive technology

Developments on the Internet changed the way people interacted with each other and consumed popular culture. They also changed the world for the corporations that produced much of that popular culture. In 2000, Internet service provider AOL and media company Time Warner merged in a huge deal.[20] They believed that they could create a "walled garden" where AOL's users would pay for music and films from Time Warner. It was one of the most disastrous miscalculations in corporate history.

AOL-Time Warner had misunderstood how the Internet was developing. Internet users did not want to be fed pop culture like they had been through radio and television in the past. People could **upload**, download, and create all sorts of new content. The idea that *anyone* could be seen or heard on the Web was one of the things that made it so revolutionary. It also had a very disruptive effect on many branches of the pop culture industry.

The way people bought popular culture also changed. Online retailers such as Amazon became big players in the markets for CDs, DVDs, and games. This caused physical music and entertainment stores to come under pressure. Shopping online even became a leisure pursuit in itself as people bought and sold through online marketplaces such as eBay.

The sale of physical items such as CDs eventually came under pressure. Digital music files were relatively easy to upload and download. Previously, people had swapped music on cassettes with poor sound quality, but music could now be swapped or listened to instantly online.

Video soon followed, with services such as YouTube offering access to a limitless variety of video. As connection speeds increased, people were able to stream films and TV programmes, whether legally or illegally. The experience of watching films on the big screen remained popular, although less popular than it had been in the past. People wondered whether television could withstand the onslaught of online content, although many TV companies launched their own "on demand" services, such as BBC iPlayer.

Illegal downloads

One of the biggest concerns for media companies was the illegal downloading of music and films. Before the Internet, most forms of commercial culture had been based on the idea that artists should be paid for the work they created. With so much content being available for free on the Internet, this concept seemed to be under threat. People wondered if this would affect the amount and quality of pop culture available.

Buying and downloading music on the Internet led to changes to physical retailers. Music shops like this were hit by declining sales, and many went out of business.

Online privacy

The "always on" online culture of the 2000s also raised questions about privacy. People posting information or photos to social networking sites often forgot that this could be viewed by all their online friends, and sometimes by strangers as well. Online, people could create whatever identities they chose as easily as typing in a false name and user profile. Unfortunately, this anonymity was also available to online criminals.

The age of celebrity

The explosion in TV channels and online media in the 2000s created more celebrities than ever before. There were also more media outlets and column inches to be filled with stories of celebrities' lives, loves, scandals, and triumphs. It is difficult to know what came first: people's fascination with celebrity or the media's glee in fuelling that obsession.

Celebrity was nothing new. Film, music, and sports stars had always been reported widely by the media. This was still the case, but a new type of celebrity was emerging, fuelled by reality TV and the growth of celebrity magazines such as *OK!* and *Heat*. There were not enough truly famous people to fill the celebrity magazines and TV channels, so people who had featured on reality TV series found themselves cast in the role of celebrity. Many of the new celebrities were "famous for being famous", but most people could not quite remember what people like Paris Hilton or the Kardashians were actually famous for.

The power of celebrity

The amount of coverage given to celebrities meant that people listened to what they had to say. Stars such as Angelina Jolie and Bono, of rock group U2, were able to use their fame to highlight good causes. Celebrity status and the resulting media interest meant that world leaders would listen to them. This was undoubtedly a good thing for the causes concerned, although many people questioned whether some celebrities were using good causes to raise their own profiles rather than the other way around. People were also concerned that less fashionable causes would suffer as a result of the obsession with celebrity **endorsement**.

Being a celebrity could even mean a route to real power, as when Hollywood icon Arnold Schwarzenegger was elected governor of California in 2003. Schwarzenegger had a long history of being involved in politics, but his celebrity status certainly helped him to be heard in the media.

Brad Pitt (1963-) and Angelina Jolie (1975-)

Brad Pitt and Angelina Jolie were two of Hollywood's biggest stars in the 2000s. Interest increased dramatically when the two became a couple in 2005. Pitt grew up in Missouri. He became one of Hollywood's brightest hopes in 1991, after appearing in *Thelma and Louise*. His varied career included starring roles in *Interview With the Vampire* (1994), *Ocean's Eleven* (2001), and *The Curious Case of Benjamin Button* (2008).

In 2000, Pitt married TV and film star Jennifer Aniston, but their marriage ended in 2005. Angelina Jolie is the daughter of actor Jon Voight. Her first major film role was in *Hackers* (1995), but her breakthrough role came as the title character in *Lara Croft: Tomb Raider* (2001). Jolie had been married twice before meeting Pitt, when they both starred in *Mr. and Mrs. Smith* (2005). The couple has six children; three were adopted from Ethiopia, Cambodia, and Vietnam. They have used their celebrity status to promote many good causes, including the plight of refugees around the world.[1]

Celebrity brands

Celebrities did not just promote good causes. Stars from sports and entertainment became the faces of many products and brands. They appeared in advertisements or actively promoted the brand at events. Sports stars including golfer Tiger Woods and footballer David Beckham earned millions endorsing sportswear companies. Celebrities from the world of entertainment could often be found endorsing clothing and cosmetics brands. Many stars, including singers Gwen Stefani and Jay-Z, launched their own clothing brands. Beyoncé was one of the highest earners from endorsements with deals to promote Nintendo and cosmetics company L'Oreal, as well as her own fashion label.[2]

Explaining the obsession

Companies that produce celebrity magazines or TV shows would say that such productions exist because they have proved to attract big audiences. Part of why we are so obsessed with celebrities is that the 24-hour media world that has grown around the Internet and multichannel TV has helped to develop this obsession. In the past, Hollywood stars and musicians could manage their public images more closely because there were fewer media outlets. People today have more access to information on celebrities, although this is often an illusion, because public appearances, interviews, and Twitter feeds are often carefully managed.

Sales of celebrity magazines boomed in the years after 2000.

This partly explains why people get so excited about scandals and problems in the lives of celebrities. When stars like singer Britney Spears struggled to deal with the glare of fame, or celebrities battled with drug or alcohol addiction, this made people even more interested in them. When celebrities make mistakes, they confirm that they are not so different from the rest of us. For the media, recovery from a setback is a better story than reporting that someone's life is great all the time. However, companies trying to sell their brands do not always see it that way. Tiger Woods lost many of his contracts due to damaging stories about his personal life.

Appearing on talk shows meant that politicians, like former British Prime Minister Tony Blair (shown on left), were less likely to face difficult questions from tough interviewers.

Celebrity and society

Celebrity culture affected many areas of society. Teachers complained that young people's education suffered because the students were tricked by the media into believing that everyone could become a celebrity, without realizing that hard work was involved.[3] Politics, which TV presenter Jay Leno once described as "show business for ugly people", was also affected as it became more about the personality of politicians. Leaders such as George W. Bush found it easier to appear on daytime TV or answer questions about his favourite cookies rather than dealing with tougher questions on policies.

Music

In June 2009, the world was shocked by the death of Michael Jackson. His tragic passing seemed like the end of an era for recorded music. Album sales had dropped so much by 2009 that it was highly unlikely that any recording would ever sell as many copies as Jackson had at his peak in the 1980s.

A new generation of listeners

The decade after the founding of Napster in 1999 was the most difficult that the music industry had ever faced. Napster allowed users to share music files online. Between 1999 and 2001, when Napster was closed down,[1] music fans got used to the idea of downloading free music online. Lots of other sites arose to replace Napster. Rather than working on a legal alternative to satisfy the demand for digital music, the music industry concentrated on closing down illegal sites and taking legal action against individual users.

At the same time that the music industry was fighting illegal downloads, other forms of entertainment were also becoming more important in people's lives. Pop music had infused society from the 1950s to the 1990s, but computers, games, and the Internet meant that, for many people, pop music no longer occupied the central place in their lives that it had for previous generations.

Younger people were also not used to the idea of buying a record or CD from a record shop and owning it. They might download it online, or they might just play the song they liked on a streaming or video site where they could hear the song but would not own it. These changing habits spelled decline for record companies, and meant the end for many physical music shops.

The growth in music downloads did not make up for declining sales of CDs.

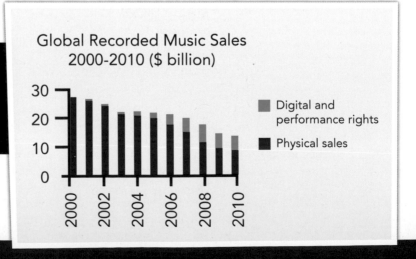

Global Recorded Music Sales 2000-2010 ($ billion)

During this time there was more music made and distributed online than ever before, from musicians with no record contract who could post their music online, to established artists such as Radiohead. As CD sales declined, vinyl records also enjoyed a revival, with buyers saying that they sounded better than CDs or digital downloads. Even so, in 2010 vinyl accounted for only one per cent of music sales in the United States, the world's largest market.[2]

Did you know?

In 2004, there were about one million songs available for legal download. By 2010, this had increased to 13 million tracks. In 2010, $4.6 billion was spent on online music.[3]

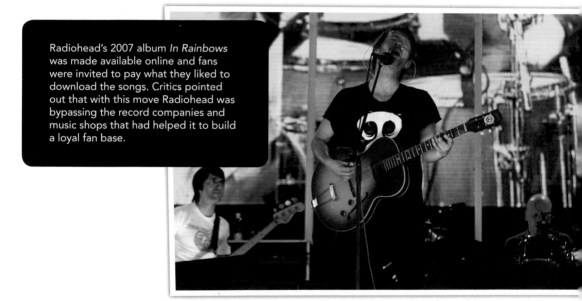

Radiohead's 2007 album *In Rainbows* was made available online and fans were invited to pay what they liked to download the songs. Critics pointed out that with this move Radiohead was bypassing the record companies and music shops that had helped it to build a loyal fan base.

The iPod

Apple's iPod was the symbol of the growth of online music. This compact and elegant device could be loaded with a record collection. People could also download tracks and albums from Apple's iTunes store. Rather than listening to songs as part of an album, iPod owners would just download tracks they liked, meaning that albums became less important.

Hip-hop

At the start of the decade, hip-hop was established in the mainstream of popular music. Like rhythm and blues in the 1950s, this African American music form had been adopted by both black and white teenagers around the world. Some hip-hop artists had often been criticized for glamourizing violence and having a dismissive attitude towards women. Their fans argued that this was the **authentic** voice of the street, but by the end of the decade rap's biggest stars were a long way from the street.

The Eminem show

The first and biggest hip-hop star of the new century was Eminem, who was a white rapper from a troubled background in Detroit. *The Marshall Mathers LP* became the fastest-selling album of all time when it was released in 2000.[4] Eminem, whose real name was Marshall Mathers, was criticized in the media for his violent and hate-filled lyrics, but was loved by his fans for his witty rhymes and confrontational personality. Despite huge sales and a string of **Grammy** awards for his albums, Eminem remained an outsider.

Hip-hop's stars produced many of the most popular records in the years after 2000. These records included the inventive and original styles of Outkast and Kanye West, Missy Elliott, the most successful female rapper, and the pop sounds of the Black Eyed Peas. But the sounds that they created also had an influence outside hip-hop. In other areas of the world hip-hop was spawning new genres, such as the grime music of Dizzee Rascal that developed in the United Kingdom.

Doing it yourself

Hip-hop and grime grew out of a do-it-yourself attitude in music in which samples of other records were used to create backing tracks. Doing it yourself was one of the features of music in the 2000s. Computer technology meant that recordings that previously would only have been possible to make in an expensive studio could now be made anywhere by anyone with a good idea and some knowledge of music. Mash-ups used sampled backing tracks and vocals to create new music, often without the permission of the original artists. Do-it-yourself music could be posted and distributed online.

Jay-Z (1970-)

Jay-Z was one of the most successful hip-hop artists of the 1990s and 2000s. He managed to combine artistic success with control of his own career and a formidable business empire. Jay-Z was born Shawn Carter in Brooklyn, New York. The kids in his neighbourhood called him Jazzy because of his smooth, laid-back personality. When he started making music, Jay-Z was determined to keep control of his career and formed Roc-a-Fella Records to release his first album in 1996. A string of successful albums followed, culminating with *The Black Album* in 2003. At that time, Jay-Z temporarily retired from music and concentrated on business ventures, including a clothing line, a film company, and a stake in an NBA basketball team. Jay-Z married R&B star Beyoncé (they are shown together above) in 2008, and they became one of the most powerful couples in pop culture.[5]

Alongside hip-hop, R&B music dominated the pop charts. Superstar producers such as the Neptunes and Timbaland came from a hip-hop background. They brought an understanding of how to add perfect beats to the good looks and pop sheen of artists such as Beyoncé and Justin Timberlake, to create popular and classy records.

Reality TV on the radio

Reality TV also produced some of the biggest hit records, particularly in the United Kingdom, where half of the 10 best-selling singles between 2000 and 2009 were sung by stars of TV shows like *X Factor*. With a few exceptions, such as Leona Lewis and Kelly Clarkson, these talent-show winners did not have lasting success after the TV shows had faded from memory. One of the most unlikely successes was Susan Boyle, a middle-aged Scottish singer who was unknown when she appeared on *Britain's Got Talent* in 2009. Boyle's debut album was the world's biggest seller in 2009.[6]

Another trend that was led by TV was interest in musical theatre, as seen in Disney's *High School Musical* and the TV series *Glee*. The combination of storylines that appealed to young viewers and well-produced musical numbers proved extremely popular. The *Glee* cast's version of Journey's 1981 song "Don't Stop Believin'" was a hit around the world in 2010. The success of Canadian teenager Justin Bieber proved that pop stars could succeed without being featured on a TV show.

As music sales declined, many musicians relied on live performances to earn a living. There was a boom in festivals, which featured lots of artists performing over several days.

Looking back

The Internet meant that music's history was never more than a mouse click away for many people. Artists and music fans alike took advantage of the availability. Many, such as the White Stripes and Arctic Monkeys, drew on the music of the past to create something that was recognizably new. Elsewhere, faces from the past such as the Eagles and the Police reunited and played the hits of earlier decades to full stadiums.

Did you know?

In 2010, the cast of *Glee* surpassed the Beatles when they became the group with the most hits on the US singles chart, the Billboard Hot 100. It took them just over a year to set this record. After each show was broadcast, songs were released online, scoring new hits every week.[7]

Lady Gaga (1986-)

When she stormed to the top of the charts in 2008, Stefani Joanne Angelina Germanotta, better known as Lady Gaga, seemed to be the ultimate twenty-first-century artist. She adapted elements from earlier eras, including the glam rock of the 1970s and the pop style of Madonna in the 1980s and 1990s. She also understood the demands of celebrity with her constant outrageous statements and outfits. Lady Gaga began performing in her native New York as a teenager. She attended music college before dropping out to pursue her career. After writing songs for artists including the Pussycat Dolls, she was signed to Interscope Records. Her albums include the optimistically titled debut *The Fame* (2008), which included the huge single "Poker Face", and *Born This Way* (2011).[8]

Design and clothes

The way people choose to design the spaces they live in is all part of popular culture. **Interior design** was another area of pop culture that looked to the past in the 2000s. A picture of a room from any decade can tell us a lot about culture and society at the time. Interior design in the 1990s had been all about space and minimalism. After 2000, people were much more likely to mix different styles from the past to create their own style, often influenced by reality TV home makeover shows.

As people became more conscious of environmental issues, it became fashionable to reuse and recycle old or "vintage" materials for new uses. The Internet continued to be an influence, as people bought and sold unwanted or valuable **retro** items on auction sites such as eBay. Caring for the environment became fashionable, as many celebrities started driving eco-friendly cars. Even politicians such as future British Prime Minister David Cameron rode bicycles to work, although Cameron was followed by a car to carry his briefcase and documents.[1]

David Cameron is shown here riding his bicycle to work in London, in 2009.

Fashion trends

Like other areas of design, fashion was more about personal style than an overall "look" of the decade. In general, people dressed less formally, including billionaire CEOs like Facebook's Mark Zuckerberg, who was often seen in a hoodie and trainers. As with so many other areas of pop culture, celebrities influenced clothing styles, as people combined main street fashion with showy, celebrity-style jewellery and designer accessories such as handbags and sunglasses.

As in many previous eras, young people's fashion was strongly influenced by other areas of popular culture, such as music and sports. Hip-hop style in particular became part of the mainstream in the early 2000s, with Jay-Z and other hip-hop stars starting their own fashion labels. The growth in popularity of extreme sports such as skateboarding inspired teenagers to wear loose-fitting, durable clothes.

The 2000s saw growing popular interest in art as demonstrated by huge visitor numbers at new museums like London's Tate Modern. Grafitti and street artists such as Banksy also began to gain more recognition in the mainstream art world. One of Banksy's spray-painted public images is shown here.

"Size zero" controversy

Fashion models like Kate Moss were some of the most recognized celebrities of the 2000s. But there was also controversy about the influence of images that young people saw of models on the catwalks of the world. Many felt that the trend for using very skinny "size zero" models encouraged young people to lose too much weight to look like these models. This might promote eating disorders. The controversy was ignited in 2006 when two South American models died as a result of eating disorders. Some fashion shows introduced restrictions on ultra-skinny models.[2]

Designing gadgets

The early years of the new century were a time of prosperity for people in the Western world. Designer handbags and sunglasses were not the only desirable accessories. Just as important was having the right phone and other gadgets. The style of these gadgets was just as important as what they actually did.

Mobile phones had become a fashion item in the late 1990s. This continued in the new decade as phones first became smaller and neater and then, as more functions and bigger screens were added, bigger again. However, phones were not the only gadgets to be transformed in the first decade of the new century. In 2000, televisions were still attached to a huge box. The development of stylish flat-screen and, later, HD televisions changed the experience of watching television, and large TV screens now took up much less space.

The right image

Digital cameras were expensive and limited at the start of the decade. The growth of digital photography and video have changed the way we take photos and films of our friends and family, and enables us to post the images online. In so many ways, these stylish gadgets have changed the way we think about pop culture.

Apple led the way in terms of design in this gadget revolution with the iPods and iPhones that sold in the millions. Products like these forced other companies to improve their own designs. Clear, accessible designs became an important feature of the best websites.

Jonathan Ive (1967-)

British designer Jonathan Ive provided the creative genius behind many of Apple's iconic products. As senior vice president and head of design with the company from 1996, he was charged with making CEO Steve Jobs's vision into functional and desirable products. Born in London, Ive was already a legendary perfectionist as a student in Newcastle. He won the Royal Society of Art's student design award twice, which recognized his potential as a young designer. In 1992, Ive moved to California to work for Apple, where he went on to design the coloured iMac, which changed how people thought a computer should look when it was launched in 1998.[3] Ive's small design team's successes in the 2000s included iPods, iPhones, and the iPad tablet computer, which launched in 2010. Ive was honoured as a commander of the British Empire in 2006,[4] a national honour marking his contribution to design.

Quote

"Next Christmas, the iPod will be dead, finished, gone, kaput."

A bold and not entirely accurate prediction from British business guru Lord Sugar, speaking in 2005.[5] Sugar's company, Amstrad, had created some of the first affordable computers, but by the 2000s he was mainly known as the star on *The Apprentice* on British TV.

Kidulthood

Having the latest gadget was vital for one pop culture trend of the 2000s – the kidult. During the later decades of the twentieth century, adults had started marrying and having children much later than they had in the 1950s and 1960s. The term *kidult* came into use as a mocking term for people who, while they were no longer young, continued to act as if they were teenagers. However, as adults they had more money for the gadgets and lifestyle that they couldn't afford when they were actually teenagers. Kidult accessories included micro-scooters, iPhones with lots of apps, game consoles, and the latest trainers.

The printed word

The world of book publishing had longer to wait than other forms of pop culture before the new technology boom changed the way people read books. Newspapers and magazines had already been battling the huge range of news and features that people could access free of charge online for many years before e-readers and tablet computers loaded with e-books started to appear.

Technology had already affected some areas of book publishing, such as travel books, as readers chose to get more of their information online. However, the 2000s also saw some of the biggest selling books of all time. Dan Brown's thriller *The Da Vinci Code* (2003) was generally agreed to be the biggest bestseller since records began.[1]

The death of newspapers?

Newspapers were first produced in the eighteenth century as a way to collate and distribute the latest events as quickly as possible, which at that time meant every day. They later developed as a great way for advertisers to sell to their customers. The World Wide Web, not to mention 24-hour TV news, could update the news every minute of the day, and it could also help advertisers reach their customers more effectively. News on the Web was also, for the most part, free. This led to a 30 per cent decline in the number of newspapers sold in the United States between 2007 and 2009. The United Kingdom fared only slightly better, with a decline of 25 per cent.[2] The story was not the same everywhere: newspapers in India boomed due to growing literacy and the lack of universal Internet access, particularly in rural areas.[3]

The celebrity memoir

Like other areas of pop culture, the book world could not resist the celebrity book. Every year, the shelves of bookstores and supermarkets groaned under the weight of the latest book by a sports star, TV star, or someone who was just famous for being famous. Many, but not all, of these books were very successful, especially if the author was particularly loved or had an interesting story to tell. Some celebrities even tried writing fiction or children's books, as Madonna did when she launched *The English Roses* in 2003, topping bestseller lists.

The birth of e-readers

In 2000, Stephen King's latest novel was published on the Web. It was downloaded by 400,000 people on the first day.[4] After the publicity had died down, e-books quietly disappeared from view. There were certainly e-books being produced, but they were mainly for academic and professional readers. Things started to change in 2006 when Sony,[5] in 2006, and Amazon,[6] in 2007, launched commercial e-readers that people could use at home and on the move. In 2010, Amazon reported that it was selling more e-books than hardback books in the United States.[7] In the same year, Apple launched its iPad tablet computer and its iBookstore.[8] E-book sales were still relatively low compared to total printed book sales, but they were here to stay.

E-readers enabled users to carry thousands of titles on a single device. Critics pointed out that a book's battery never died.

Harry Potter

The most successful author of the 2000s was undoubtedly J. K. Rowling. The first three of the seven titles in the *Harry Potter* series about the adventures of a boy wizard were published in the 1990s, but it was in the 2000s that the series became a publishing success story like no other. By the time all seven titles had been published in 2008, the series had sold more than 375 million copies in 63 languages.[9] The popularity of the series was boosted by the blockbuster films of each book in the series, which broke records in their own right and made stars of their leading actors Daniel Radcliffe and Emma Watson.

Did you know?

In 2001, the *New York Times* introduced a separate bestseller list for children's books after *Harry Potter* had filled the first three spots on their main bestseller list for more than a year.[10]

J. K. Rowling (1965-)

Joanne Rowling became one of the most recognized faces of the twenty-first century. She was born in Chipping Sodbury, near Bristol, UK. It was on a train journey from London to Manchester in 1990 that Rowling first came up with the idea for Harry Potter. "I simply sat and thought," she recalled later, "for four (delayed train) hours... and this scrawny, black-haired, bespectacled boy who didn't know he was a wizard became more and more real to me."[11] *Harry Potter and the Philosopher's Stone* took a long time to write because Rowling was also caring for her eldest daughter Jessica, born in 1993. The book was finally published in 1997.[12] Interest grew gradually and, by 2000, the first three *Harry Potter* books filled the top three spots on the *New York Times* bestseller list.

The *Harry Potter* series, the most successful example of young adult fiction, appealed not just to teenagers but adults also. The next subject to achieve big success was the vampire novel, in particular the *Twilight* saga, written by Stephenie Meyer. As with *Harry Potter*, the successful books were inevitably followed by a series of films, starring Robert Pattinson and Kristen Stewart.

Graphic novels were another genre that achieved success with young readers in the 2000s, with authors such as Neil Gaiman producing exciting and sophisticated publications. Films such as *The Dark Knight* (2008) also helped to increase interest in graphic novels.

Teenage magazines

Film stars such as Robert Pattinson have always been a big feature of teenage magazines, which cover entertainment and other lifestyle issues. The sales of teenage magazines were affected by technology and other changes during this period. Much of the material these magazines traditionally covered was available online, along with video and other features. Teenage and adult markets began to merge, as teenagers started to read celebrity magazines aimed at adults or magazines dealing with particular interests such as gaming or sports.

Stephenie Meyer's *Twilight* saga made vampires into attractive and romantic figures rather than the bloodsucking killers of traditional vampire films and books.

edward

twilight

Pop culture turned upside down?

Pop culture is not just a feature of Western countries such as North America, Europe, and Australia, although US pop culture in particular dominated the world during most of the twentieth century. As Western countries struggled through economic problems after 2007, many Asian countries continued to become more prosperous. People had more money to spend than before, and this led to dramatic growth in homegrown popular culture.

Around the world

Korean music, films, and TV gained popularity across Asia and increasingly in Asian communities living in North America and Europe. K-pop, as Korean music is known, features bands such as Kara and Super Junior. China's media is closely controlled by the state, but prosperity has led to more demand for both homegrown and foreign pop culture.

Japan continued to be receptive to Western popular music and culture, which was often given a distinctly Japanese twist. The Japanese manga style of illustration in comic books became popular around the world.

As with so much of pop culture, the Internet drove much of the spread of culture around the world, with music and video available globally through YouTube and other websites. While this helped the spread of Western pop culture, it also helped the growth of local and regional pop culture in markets such as Asia.

Latin American pop culture

Like English, Spanish is one of the most widely spoken languages in the world. Popular culture produced in Spanish-speaking Latin America can be sold throughout the region, and is particularly popular with the large Spanish-speaking population of the United States. The US TV show *Ugly Betty* was based on a Colombian show.[1] Latin American music, particularly from Brazil and Cuba, has also had a big influence around the world, with Latin American dance music proving particularly popular.

Did you know?

One of the reasons for the film *Avatar's* global success was that it was the most successful film of all time in China. China restricts the number of foreign films that can be shown in the country each year.[2]

Takeshi Kaneshiro (1973-)

Takeshi Kaneshiro was one of the most popular celebrities in southeast Asia during the 1990s and 2000s. As the star of a huge range of films, Kaneshiro has been called "the Brad Pitt of Asia".[3] Kaneshiro's father was Japanese, and his mother came from Taiwan. He spent his childhood in Taiwan but attended Japanese school and never felt fully Taiwanese. He has made films in several Asian countries, made possible by his ability to speak five languages. Kaneshiro began his career as a teenage pop star but later admitted that he couldn't sing. As an actor, he was able to play a huge range of characters from romantic leads to ancient Chinese warriors. Kaneshiro's most famous films include *House of Flying Daggers* (2004) and *Red Cliff* (2007). One reason for his popularity across southeast Asia is that he remains mysterious, because little is known about his life away from the screen.[4]

What did the 2000s do for us?

The changing face of pop culture usually reflects changes in the wider society, and the first decade of the twenty-first century was no exception to that rule. As people became more prosperous in Asia and other parts of the world, pop culture grew and changed with them. However, as we have seen throughout this book, it was technology and the Internet that changed pop culture forever during this era.

Technology: positives and negatives

Advances in technology meant that artists could create amazing CGI and special effects in films like *Avatar*. At the other end of the scale, technology helped independent artists to create films and music using technology that was widely available online or in many stores.

However, the Internet also created changes that many people were less comfortable with. Illegal downloading of music and films meant that artists and producers who created them did not get paid. As of 2010, only 44 per cent of US Internet users thought that they should pay for music, and it has been estimated that, despite the success of paid services like iTunes, around 90 per cent of music downloads are illegal.[1]

Multichannel culture

Many of the biggest cultural phenomena of the era were presented through various media. A successful book or graphic novel might be turned into a film and a video game. TV programmes would feature music that could be released on CD and online. Blockbuster films featured pop stars and were often organized in series so that sequels would have a guaranteed audience. None of these techniques were new – Elvis Presley and the Beatles had appeared in films in the 1950s and 1960s – but the marketing of pop culture seemed to reach new levels of sophistication after 2000. Of course there were always independent films and musicians to react against what many viewed as the bland branding of pop culture.

Closing the generation gap

Since pop culture first started to be produced for teenagers in the 1950s, there had usually been a generation gap in the pop culture enjoyed by young people and older generations. In the 2000s this changed slightly, as adults and young people alike read *Harry Potter* and listened to music from TV shows such as *The X Factor* and *Glee*.

The new pop culture moguls

In the past, major publishers, film, and music companies could control the popular culture that was created and distributed. Changes in pop culture would often come from smaller independent companies taking chances on new artists or genres. In the 2000s, anyone could create pop culture and distribute it through the Web. The new pop culture moguls were companies such as Apple, Amazon, and Google, who controlled so much of what we found and bought online. These companies also collected lots of information about what we chose to watch or search for online. This enabled them to make suggestions of other things we might like, but many people thought it undermined our privacy.

For the first time most people no longer needed a record company to make a recording, and they could get it heard online through services such as MySpace.

Where do we go from here?

It is very difficult to try to predict what will happen in pop culture in the next 10 or 20 years. Most of the major developments in pop culture were not predicted at the time. For example, most people in 2000 would not have predicted the huge changes in the music industry or the steep decline of newspapers. No one could have foreseen the amazing success of *Harry Potter* when the first book was published in 1997.

In the future, more pop culture will be accessed on mobile devices such as smartphones.

Technology will undoubtedly continue to change the way people make and consume pop culture, creating new visual effects in films and even more realistic and sophisticated video games. This may result in blockbuster films being more and more expensive to make, meaning that there will be fewer made and companies will be biased towards surefire hits such as sequels to popular films. *Pirates of the Caribbean Part 8* could be with us by 2020!

As we saw in the 2000s, the number and speed of connections to the Internet will continue to grow in the future. This will affect other media such as television and radio, with events such as concerts and other pop culture being viewed over the Internet, or on Internet-connected TV, rather than through traditional broadcasting. In this age of truly global communication, stars and culture from India and China will become more important. Pop culture trends and fads will also spread around the world much more quickly.

Backlash?

As developments in technology continue to dominate new pop culture trends, there may be a backlash of people looking to revive forms of culture that can be seen as more local or authentic, such as locally based film and TV industries rather than global mega-franchises. Along with these changes, there are bound to be many others that we cannot predict.

Museum pieces?

Will we still be talking about the following things in 2020, or will we only see them in museums?

- DVDs: In 2000, video cassettes were still the preferred way of watching films at home. Within a few years they had been replaced by DVDs. But will downloads replace the DVD and even high-definition Blu-ray discs?
- Record shops: Will there still be people buying CDs and records in actual shops, or will all music be bought online?
- Hardback books: Hardback editions were normally published before paperbacks at a higher price. Will e-books replace hardbacks? Will paperback books survive?
- 3-D films: Not all the changes that occurred in pop culture in the 2000s will become established. Is 3-D a passing fad or a permanent part of the film industry?

Timeline

Year	Popular culture	World events
2000	Sony launches PlayStation 2. Reality TV show *Big Brother* appears on US and UK TV for the first time. Eminem, *The Marshall Mathers LP* (music).	Dot-com boom in Internet companies peaks.
2001	File sharing service Napster is closed down by legal action from music companies. Apple launches iPod music player. Launch of online encyclopedia *Wikipedia*. *Lord of the Rings: The Fellowship of the Ring* (film).	George W. Bush becomes US president. (11 September) Terrorists attack New York and Washington by flying hijacked planes into buildings.
2002	*Pop Idol* TV show launched in United Kingdom. *American Idol* TV show launched in United States. Halle Berry becomes the first African American to win the Oscar for Best Actress.	
2003	Jay-Z, *The Black Album* (music).	Hollywood star Arnold Schwarzenegger is elected governor of California.
2004	Launch of *World of Warcraft*, the most successful MMORPG. Launch of Facebook. *Fahrenheit 9/11* (Documentary film).	(26 December) More than 200,000 people die in the Indian Ocean tsunami.

2005	Stephenie Meyer, *Twilight* (novel). DVD sales become Hollywood's biggest source of revenue.	(7 July) Terrorists attack underground trains and a bus in London. Hurricane Katrina causes widespread flooding in New Orleans, Louisiana.
2006	Brad Pitt and Angelina Jolie meet while filming *Mr. and Mrs. Smith*. PlayStation 3 and Nintendo Wii launched. Verb to *google* enters Oxford English Dictionary.	Execution of former Iraqi leader Saddam Hussein.
2007	Launch of Twitter. Radiohead release album *In Rainbows* as a download available from their website.	
2008	Amazon launches Kindle e-book reader. Lady Gaga, *The Fame* (music).	(September) Collapse of Lehman Brothers triggers global economic crisis.
2009	Bollywood-inspired *Slumdog Millionaire* wins Oscar for Best Picture. *Avatar* (film).	Barack Obama becomes US president.
2010	Reality TV star Susan Boyle's debut album is the best-selling record of the year. The cast of *Glee* overtakes the Beatles as the artists who have had the most recordings on *Billboard* Hot 100 in the United States. *The Social Network* (film).	David Cameron leads new coalition government in the United Kingdom.

Index

actors 10, 12, 13, 14, 15, 18, 27, 30, 31, 46, 49
advertising 16, 18, 22, 24, 32, 44
African Americans 7, 9, 12, 13, 36, 37
Amazon 28, 45, 51
America's Army (video game) 21
animated films 10, 11
AOL-Time Warner 28
Apple Computers 5, 23, 26, 35, 42, 45, 51
Avatar (film) 11, 49, 50

Beyoncé 32, 37, 38
Bieber, Justin 38
Big Brother (television show) 18
Bin Laden, Osama 6
blockbusters 10–11, 46, 50, 53
blogs 23, 24, 27
Blu-ray disks 53
Bollywood 14, 15
books 10, 12, 23, 44, 45, 46–47, 50, 52, 53
Boyle, Susan 38
Brown, Dan 44
Bush, George W. 6, 9, 33

cable television 16
Call of Duty series 21
Cameron, David 40
celebrities 23, 30, 31, 32–33, 39, 40, 41, 45, 47, 49
celebrity magazines 30, 32, 47
censorship 9, 48
children's books 12, 45, 46–47
climate change 8
clothing 8, 32, 37, 41, 42
comic books 48
Computer Generated Imagery (CGI) 10, 50
Cowell, Simon 19
Cyrus, Miley 17

dance 14, 18, 48
The Da Vinci Code (Dan Brown) 44
Depp, Johnny 12
digital cameras 42
Digital Versatile Discs (DVDs) 8, 10, 11, 16, 20, 28, 53
Digital Video Recorders 16
documentaries 12, 18

eating disorders 41
eBay 23, 28, 40
e-books 45, 53
e-commerce 6, 23, 28, 35, 40, 45, 50, 51
economies 6, 7, 8, 48
Eminem 36

Facebook 23, 24, 25, 41
fashion. See clothing.
file sharing 16, 28, 34, 50
film industry 7, 9, 10–11, 12, 13, 14, 15, 16, 17, 25, 28, 30, 31, 46, 47, 48, 49, 50, 51, 53
fossil fuels 8

game consoles 20–21
Glee (television show) 38, 39, 50
globalization 8
Google Inc. 22, 23, 51
Gore, Al 12
graphic novels 47, 50
greenhouse gases 8
grime music 36

Harry Potter series 11, 12, 46–47, 50, 52
hip-hop music 13, 36, 37, 38, 41
Hussein, Saddam 6

interior design 40
Internet 5, 6, 8, 9, 16, 18, 21, 22, 24, 27, 28, 32, 34, 36, 39, 40, 44, 48, 50, 53
iPads 42, 45
iPhones 5, 26, 42, 43
iPods 26, 35, 42, 43
iTunes 35, 50
Ive, Jonathan 42

Jackson, Michael 34
Jay-Z 32, 37, 41
Jolie, Angelina 12, 30, 31

Kaneshiro, Takeshi 49
"kidults" 43
King, Stephen 45
K-pop music 48

Lady Gaga 39
Latin American music 48
Leno, Jay 33
literature 10, 12, 23, 44, 45, 46–47, 50, 52, 53
The Lord of the Rings trilogy 10
Lord Sugar 43

Madonna 39, 45
magazines 24, 30, 32, 44, 47
makeover shows 18, 40
Manga 48
The Marshall Mathers LP 36
mash-ups 36
memes 27
Meyer, Stephenie 47
MMORPGs (Massively Multi-player Online Role-playing Games) 21
mobile phones 5, 8, 26, 27, 42, 43
Moore, Michael 12
Moss, Kate 41
motion capture technology, 10, 11
movies. See film industry.
Murdoch, Rupert 24
music 12, 13, 14, 17, 18, 19, 21, 26, 28, 30, 32, 34–35, 36, 37, 38, 39, 41, 48, 50, 51, 52
musicals 38, 39
MySpace 24

Napster 34
newspapers 23, 44, 52
news programmes 44

Obama, Barack 7, 9, 24
online gaming 21

Pattinson, Robert 12, 47
Pitt, Brad 12, 31
pollution 8
privacy 29, 51

Radcliffe, Daniel 12, 46
radio 16, 28, 53
Radiohead (musical group) 35
Rai, Aishwarya 14, 15
Rascal, Dizzee 36
reality television 18, 19, 30, 38, 40
rhythm and blues (R&B) music 36, 37, 38
Rowling, J. K. 46

sampling 36
satellites 16
Schwarzenegger, Arnold 30
search engines 22
September 11 attacks 6, 7, 12
Serkis, Andy 10
smartphones 5, 8, 26, 42, 43
Smith, Will 12, 13
The Social Network (film) 25
social networks 23, 24, 25, 29
special effects 10, 50, 53
sport 21, 30, 32, 33, 41, 45, 47
Spurlock, Morgan 12

tablet computers 42, 44, 45
teenage magazines 47
television 8, 10, 12, 13, 14, 16, 17, 18, 19, 24, 28, 30, 32, 33, 38, 40, 42, 43, 44, 48, 50, 53
terrorism 6, 7, 12
text messages 18, 26
three-dimensional (3-D) movies 11, 17, 53
Tolkien, J. R. R. 10
Twilight series 47
Twitter 24, 32

Ugly Betty (television show) 48

videocassettes 16, 53
video games 20–21, 34, 50, 53

war on terror 6, 7
Watson, Emma 46
Wikipedia 23
Woods, Tiger 32, 33
World Wide Web 22, 23, 24, 26, 28, 42, 44, 45, 48, 51

X Factor (television show) 18, 19, 38, 50

YouTube 22, 23, 24, 27, 28, 48

Zuckerberg, Mark 24, 25, 41